THEY'RE WATCHING YOU

Personal Privacy on Social Media

Alexis Burling

Enslow Publishing
101 W. 23rd Street
Suite 240
New York, NY 10011
USA

enslow.com

Published in 2020 by Enslow Publishing, LLC.
101 W. 23rd Street, Suite 240, New York, NY 10011

Library of Congress Cataloging-in-Publication Data

Names: Burling, Alexis, author.
Title: They're watching you : personal privacy on social media / Alexis Burling.
Description: New York : Enslow Publishing, 2020. | Series: Social media smarts | Audience: Grade 5-8. | Includes bibliographical references and index.
Identifiers: LCCN 2018055196| ISBN 9781978507784 (library bound) | ISBN 9781978507777 (paperback)
Subjects: LCSH: Social media—Security measures—Juvenile literature. | Online social networks—Security measures—Juvenile literature.
Classification: LCC HM742 .B88 2020 | DDC 302.3—dc23
LC record available at https://lccn.loc.gov/2018055196

Printed in the United States of America

To Our Readers: We have done our best to make sure all website addresses in this book were active and appropriate when we went to press. However, the author and the publisher have no control over and assume no liability for the material available on those websites or on any websites they may link to. Any comments or suggestions can be sent by email to customerservice@enslow.com.

Photo Credits: Cover, p. 1 Ljupco Smokovski/Shutterstock.com; p. 5 Nopparat Khokthong/Shutterstock.com; p. 6 pujislab/Shutterstock.com; pp. 7, 32, 40 Rawpixel.com/Shutterstock.com; p. 10 Kolonko/Shutterstock.com; p. 12 TrifonenkoIvan/Shutterstock.com; p. 15 Kostsov/Shutterstock.com; p. 19 silverkblackstock/Shutterstock.com; p. 22 Rzt_Moster/Shutterstock.com; p. 24 solarseven/Shutterstock.com; p. 27 Peter Dazeley/Photographer's Choice/Getty Images; p. 30 MicroOne/Shutterstock.com; p. 35 Blan-k/Shutterstock.com; p. 38 M-Sur/Shutterstock.com.

Contents

Introduction

Imagine what your life would be like without social media. No more streaming videos on YouTube. No more showing off snazzy outfits or posting cool photos of stuff you love on Instagram. No more instant messaging with pals on Snapchat. Life would be totally boring, right?

Thankfully, that's not going to happen anytime soon. Social media is here to stay. In fact, more people are jumping on the social media bandwagon than ever before—especially teens. According to a 2018 Pew Research Center study, 45 percent of teens in the United States are online "almost constantly." About 85 percent use YouTube, 72 percent use Instagram, and 69 percent use Snapchat. Only 3 percent of teens claim they don't use social media at all.[1]

But just because social media has been embraced by teens (and seemingly every other age group on the planet), that doesn't mean it doesn't cause problems. One of the biggest concerns facing all social media users today is the issue of privacy. Who has access to our personal data and how are they using it? Do we have any real control over our online

With a mobile device on your desk, in your bag, or tucked inside your pocket basically 24-7, it's no wonder you and your pals are online almost constantly. Hello, easy access?

presence? Even if we make our profiles private, does what we post there actually *stay* private?

Unfortunately, the wishy-washy answer to that last question is sort of, but not always—and even then, not really. If you post a slideshow on Facebook of you and your BFFs partying on the beach during spring break in Florida, there's a good chance that your friends, your friends of friends, and maybe even those friends of friends' grandparents or a future boss might see it. What's more, thanks to things like analytic software and ad-tracking programs, big corporations have access, too. Companies hoping to market products to you can mine your search habits. Then they can post advertisements on your feed based on your tastes. (If you noticed a flurry of ads for bathing suits after doing some online shopping for warm-weather clothes, that might be the reason why.)

But don't worry. You're not doomed to a full-on invasion of the privacy snatchers the minute you create an Instagram profile. And, just because you use social media doesn't mean you have to be totally on board with your deets being "out

Aren't you looking fab on the beach? Posting selfies on social media is totally cool. But make sure those pics are Grandma- or future boss–approved and don't reveal any personal info.

Reign supreme over your social media domain by staying on top of your privacy game. Learn the know-how. Kick Internet predators to the curb!

there" for everyone to see. There are updatable settings on smartphone apps and foolproof emergency procedures you can put in place in case a privacy breach occurs. There are a number of ways to protect not only your personal data but your sanity as well.

In this book, you'll learn the difference between the public and private you. We'll also go over why knowing the difference between the two is important. You'll find oodles of (hopefully) helpful tips on how to keep your online footprint wacky and fun while staying safe and responsible. We'll also walk you through all the nitty-gritty details about how to choose secure passwords, what phishing (and smishing!) is, and how to deactivate your profile if you've been a victim of identity theft.

We know. Some of you might find all this talk about privacy a bit scary. But think of it this way: Knowing all the facts means you're taking full ownership of your social media presence. You have the power to keep predators away. What could be more empowering than that?

The Private vs. Public You

In a perfect world, you could post anything online without thinking about the consequences. You could upload a video of Saturday night's slumber party to YouTube for all of your friends (and crushes) to see. Or dash out a sarcastic comment on Facebook about something that happened to your frenemy at school. You could even "like" a politically themed (but ethically questionable) meme that went viral on Twitter. The world is your oyster, right?

But many sociologists and other experts believe that being free and easy on social media isn't actually the smartest move. In minor cases it can reinforce poor decision-making habits, especially when "likes" and followers become your go-to for measuring your popularity. (We totally swear: the number of "likes" your pic gets on Instagram *is not a measure of how many friends you have!*) "Teens can quickly get caught up in the feedback loop, posting and sharing images and videos that they believe will gain the largest reaction," says Ana

Homayoun, author of *Social Media Wellness: Helping Teens and Tweens Thrive in an Unbalanced Digital World*. "Over time, teens' own values may become convoluted within an online world of instantaneous feedback, and their behavior online can become based on their 'all about the likes' values rather than their real-life values."[1]

In more serious circumstances, opening up too much online, even to close friends and family, can lead to embarrassing or dangerous situations. A sexy photo you send to your crush could be captured in a screen grab and circulated to the whole

Favorites, hearts, and likes on social media are super addictive. But don't believe the thumbs-up hype! As in most offline situations, likes don't always equal love.

school as a joke. (No, we don't think it's funny either.) An offhand comment about where you live, when combined with other information like your Social Security number, can lead to stalking. Or worse, identity theft by a complete stranger.

Of course, the last thing we want to do is spook you. But it's important to know how to tell the difference between what's fine to share publicly and what you definitely want to keep private. There are lots of ways to be smart about how you present yourself and interact with others on social media— while still having fun. A great place to start is by being aware of your digital footprint.

Beware Your Digital Footprint

Your digital footprint is all the information about you that appears online. Think about it this way: Your footsteps leave an actual trail on the ground where you have walked. What you post online leaves a digital trail, too. Everything you do makes a statement about who you are and what you stand for. A picture or post you think is funny and harmless today could be seen and misunderstood by people you have never met tomorrow.

Take the sexy photo. That's a perfect example of something that should be kept between you and the person to whom you sent the photo—and no one else. The same logic holds true for videos, Snapchat messages, and your opinionated rants on a friend's private Instagram feed. Burn this into your brain:

Anything can be forwarded and circulated widely, even if it's a text or comment meant for one person. Why? Screenshots, of course! So if you don't want a college admissions officer seeing it, the safest course of action is don't post it.

Need some basic ground rules? How about this: When unsure, keep it pure! Be kind to others. Don't be a troll and post

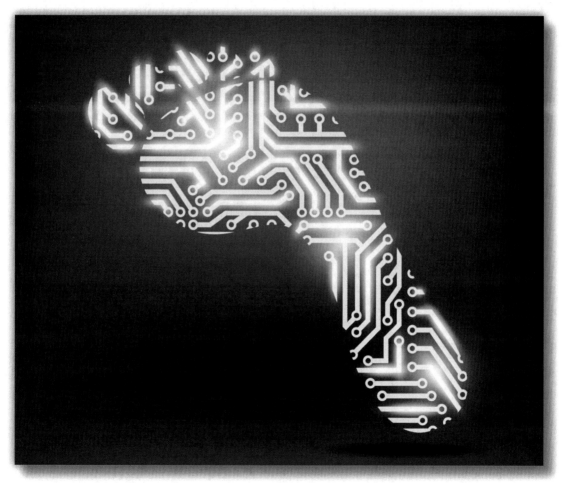

Your digital footprint is all the information about you that appears online. Work to keep it squeaky clean and above board at all times.

hurtful comments on other users' profiles or even on online message boards. After all, dishing out snarky observations (even "liking" others' questionable content) reflects poorly on your reputation. Racist, sexist, and politically incorrect remarks, or any type of commentary that can be construed by someone as offensive, is always off limits. Period.

But protecting your digital footprint isn't just about being mindful of your own activity on social media. It's also about being aware of *others'* habits, too. If your friend posts a video without asking of a private hangout you had at your house over the weekend, it could hurt the feelings of pals who weren't invited. There's also a bigger privacy issue at stake that involves not just you but your family or guardians as well. That video contains details about what's inside your home, including any valuables. If it got into the wrong hands, it could attract unwanted attention from thieves.

When a friend or someone you know is acting in a way you're not kosher with on social media, don't ignore the problem. Ask them to take down the post. If they won't, talk to a guardian or teacher who can help take care of the issue. If that doesn't work, contact the site's administrator to have the post blocked or removed.

Safeguard Your Deets

When creating and shaping your digital footprint, think of the process like keeping a diary. You wouldn't share its contents with the entire school population, right? The same argument exists for posting personal deets on social media.

Private information should be kept private. That means don't share your home street address, phone number, email address, Social Security number, bank account info, usernames and passwords, or any other important information that could be used without your knowledge. Even information about where you go to school or which classes you take is considered super risky posting material by most experts (and parents!).

Geotagging is another potentially tricky habit. This practice involves "tagging" a geographical location to something like a status update, a tweet, a video, or some other thing you post online. It gives your friends and followers a deeper look into where you are and what you're doing at the exact moment of your post. Many teens swear this isn't a weird thing to do. After all, it pings pals who might want to meet up while you're on the go. But it also provides a way for anyone—and yes, we mean anyone—to find you or track your whereabouts.

Think of it this way. Tagging yourself when you're out lets people know you're not home. If you're on a family vacay, do you really want *everyone in the world with internet access* knowing your house is empty? People have been burglarized this way—even Kim Kardashian learned to keep her location more secret after being robbed in Paris.

Geotagging is super convenient. But is it safe? Not so much. According to the *New York Times*, companies mine geotagging data from more than 200 million mobile devices in the United States.

Activate Privacy Settings

Aside from just saying no to geotagging, one of the most important actions you can take to protect yourself online is to pay attention to privacy settings. All social media apps have them. By swiping a few buttons to the right, you can control which posts you want different groups of people to see and how your information is used.

"Rinsta" vs. "Finsta"

In the world of social media, it can be tricky to tell the difference between what's meant for public consumption and the stuff that should be guarded. But many teens have figured out a solution. On Instagram, some teens have two profiles. One is their public account ("rinsta"). The other ("finsta") is for friends only.[2]

Other teens use specific apps to protect their content. One is called Vaulty. It allows users to hide photos and videos in secret storage vaults. Users can create two passwords for one vault. Each password comes with a different level of access. Vaulty also has a "mug shot" feature. It snaps a picture of anyone who tries to access the app using an incorrect password.

The safest setting is private mode. This restricts your photos and posts (and, yes, geotags) to only people who are in your personal circle. In some apps like Facebook, you can separate viewers into friends, friends of friends, and the public and decide who can see certain types of personal information, such as your birthday. You can also control whether your profile shows up in search engine results, like Google.

But as we hinted at earlier, even these safeguards aren't 100 percent fail-safe. "Information shared within a private group can be easily captured in a screenshot and shared with a wider audience," says Ana Homayoun.[3] "The notion of privacy online is only as reliable as teens' relationships with other users, and that combined with general privacy concerns provides little guarantee that online information will ever be kept secret."[4]

The best you can do is to take *all* possible precautions. You can totally continue to have fun. Promise! You just need to be thoughtful about it! And remember: if you encounter a problem, contact an adult who can take the next steps to help you stay safe.

Marketing and Data Mining

Raise your hand if you like shopping for cool stuff at the mall. (Duh, who doesn't?) How about buying things like a super fly pair of Madewell jeans or the latest *Fortnite* video game online? (Another no-brainer.) But after jamming out on your online purchase, have you also noticed ads for related products taking control of your screen the next time you hop on the web?

Unfortunately in today's tech-dependent world, targeted ads have become a super annoying reality. The reason? Companies like H&M, Best Buy, and even Amazon are actually *watching* you. They're keeping track of your spending habits in order to send you information about similar products in the hopes that you'll buy them.

While the practice may seem super invasive, the same thing happens on social media. The process is called social media mining. It occurs when companies and organizations secretly collect data about people on social media. Then they analyze it in order to form conclusions about users and

Have you noticed targeted ads popping up in your social media feeds? One culprit is your online shopping habits. Companies see what you buy and want to sell you more, more, more!

their communities. The information is then used in marketing campaigns for anything from total-slayage Leona platform boots to hunky LeBron James advertisements in subway stations during the NBA playoffs.

But that's not all your tweets, favorites, and likes are used for. Political campaigns hire huge data-mining companies to search millions of social media accounts. These "big data" firms look for patterns between users of a certain age, sex, ethnic group, or geographic location. Then they figure out how a specific population might feel about certain issues. The companies also use that data to post targeted pop-ads on users' social media feeds to try to influence users' votes.

Does all of this data-mining mumbo jumbo seem a little confusing? Believe us, we're right there with you. Let's take a look at each segment a bit more closely in order to understand what you're up against.

Marketing Mayhem

According to a 2018 Pew Research Center study, 95 percent of teens ages thirteen to seventeen own a smartphone.[1] Unless you are bending over backwards to customize it, your phone is tracking your movements by default. That means it's automatically sending companies information on where you live, the restaurants you frequent, and the physical or online stores where you shop.

What's more, many social media and other apps you've downloaded may be taking the same types of information and sharing it with third parties, depending on the privacy settings you've chosen. For example, let's say you're searching for a new pair of Adidas kicks. You might post a link to the shoes you're interested in buying on Instagram. Through its partnership with Instagram, Adidas might gain access to that information and send you ads based on your browsing habits. Instagram states this on its site: "Partners provide information about your activities off Facebook—including information about your device, websites you visit, purchases you make, the ads you see, and how you use their services… We use the information we have about you—including information about your interests, actions and connections—to select and personalize ads, offers and other sponsored content that we show you."[2]

These made-especially-for-you ads are convenient, sure—especially if Adidas posts a pic of the exact shoes you want. Bonus! But let's be clear. You didn't hand over your info willingly. Because of its partnership with Insta, Adidas technically snuck a peak at your feed without asking.

So how do you banish these ads from your life once and for all? More important, how do you stop Big Data from putting its grubby fingerprints all over your private info? Social media sites, along with most other websites, use things called cookies to track your online search habits and preferences. A bit like breadcrumbs (or, well, cookie crumbs), cookies are encrypted text files. Web servers pass those files on to your web browser each time you visit a website. They also do things like store order information and remember your passwords to make your life easier. If you disable these cookies, companies can't drop tracking devices onto your computer. On the other hand, these same sites will not be able to remember your preferences—and that includes hard-to-remember passwords.

But don't fret yet. As with many tech-related conundrums, there's another path forward. All social media platforms and

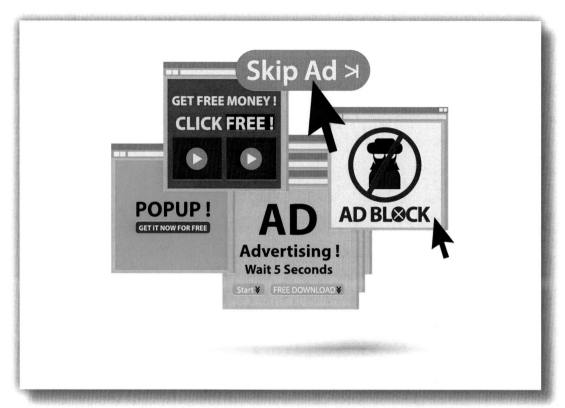

Clicking on unknown links can not only cause pesky ads to infiltrate your social media feeds, it can also harm your computer's hard drive. When in doubt: DON'T CLICK.

legit websites are legally obligated to explain if and how they use users' data. So first off, make sure you examine these sites' privacy policies *before* you reveal any of your personal 411. If anything's confusing, ask an adult to explain the small print. If you're at all uncomfortable, go to your app's privacy settings and opt out of any data-sharing opportunities whenever possible.

Second, limit the number of times you click on the ads you see on social media or elsewhere, no matter what they are for.

Clicking on one will lead to more—like acne on your forehead. Pretty soon, you'll be up to your eyeballs in pop-ups from companies you've never even heard of. In some cases, this can lead to unwanted emails, catalog mailings, or other junk mail sent to your home. Truth. We totally feel your pain. The whole shebang sounds beyond time-consuming. But you'll rest easy-peasy once you've taken the appropriate actions to ensure your data stays protected.

Private Politics

Now let's talk politics. As your parent, guardian, or teacher might have explained to you, social media played a huge role in the 2016 US presidential election. Not all of the facts have

Malware vs. Spyware vs. Scareware

If you have access to a computer, one of the most important steps you should take is to get antivirus software installed to protect your hard drive—and your data—from harm. The software fights threats from malware, spyware, and other bugs. Malware is just an easier way of saying malicious software.[3] Spyware is a type of malware that spies on your computer and steals your passwords or other personal information. Eek! Be especially careful of scareware. These programs don't protect your security. In fact, some companies use shady tactics to "scare" you into buying their product. When you do, the scareware steals your info!

Malware, spyware, scareware, and other types of viruses are lethal to your computer or mobile device. If your tech has been infected, get help from a professional immediately.

been determined. But experts suspect Russian hackers used millions of Facebook and Instagram accounts to influence the outcome of the election. They stole users' data and posed as Americans on social media. Then the Russians used these fake profiles to distribute untrue ads and post vexing images. "Facebook built incredibly effective tools which let Russia profile citizens here in the U.S. and figure out how to manipulate us," says Jonathan Albright, research director at Columbia University's Tow Center for Digital Journalism. "Facebook, essentially, gave them everything they needed."[4]

In the next chapter, we'll discuss what hacking is in more detail. We'll also go into how to best prevent things like identity theft and phishing scams from happening. But when it comes to politics and social media, there are a few rules of thumb to keep in your noggin. Some tips to follow:

- Be wary of what you post when it comes to politics. In this day and age, it's a heated subject. You never know who is reading your posts or how what you write might be interpreted. Always avoid direct or indirect attacks on a person's race, gender, religion, or political beliefs.

- Be aware that what you post online could be seen by political parties or other companies. And they could use it to their advantage. If you don't want to be marketed to by Republicans, Democrats, or any other political organizations, keep your political convos offline.

- If you manage a blog or presence on YouTube, Facebook, or Twitter in addition to your personal account, act responsibly. Protect not only the information you post about yourself, but keep others' info on the DL, too.

- If you notice suspicious activity, tell an adult right away *and* contact the site's administrator immediately. We know we sound like a broken record on this one. But your privacy—and that of all people in the United States and around the world—is important.

Hacking, Phishing, and Identity Theft

Here's something from Captain Obvious: the internet is amazing. It's now more possible than ever to find information—about pretty much anything—online. Because of the increasing popularity of social media, we can seamlessly connect with family, friends, and even strangers we don't know but want to meet anywhere in the world.

But this exhilarating freedom comes with a downside. With so many people's personal details available online, there's a much greater likelihood that at least some of it could be snatched and used for malicious purposes. A particularly shocking example is Facebook's 2018 security breach. In September of that year, the private data of nearly 50 million users was exposed. It was the largest attack in the company's fourteen-year history. The attackers, called hackers, manipulated an aspect of Facebook's code to access users' profiles in order to potentially take control of them. That's on top of an even bigger breach in 2017 when a British data-mining firm got its fingers on upwards of 87 million users'

If you fall victim to identity theft, it can be very difficult to fix the problem. Hackers can go years without being identified. In fact, some scammers are never caught.

data.[1] When a greedy hacker or other untrustworthy swindler steals your private information and illegally uses it to obtain cash or credit, this is called identity theft. According to a 2018 study, there were 16.7 million victims of identity theft in 2017. Of that number, 13,852 of thefts involved children and teens under nineteen.[2]

We know what you're thinking. Why are kids and teens, of all people, so targeted by thieves? The answer is weirdly simple:

young people usually have squeaky-clean credit scores. After all, most of you have never taken out credit, don't have debt, or haven't been late with a payment. Who *wouldn't* want to be you, right? The worst part is, after your oh-so-pristine identity is hijacked, it is then used to steal *more* people's information. Your Social Security number can also be used for opening credit card and bank accounts, taking out loans, or renting a place to live.

Having your social media and other accounts hacked and your identity stolen is psychologically scarring, for sure. It's also very time-consuming and can sometimes take months, if not years, to successfully complete Operation Damage Control. In order to prevent the nightmare from occurring (or reoccurring ad nauseam), there are two ultra-important first steps to take.

Watch Out for Phishing

Phishing sounds like a made-up word. But it's actually a pretty common practice. It's when a stranger poses as someone you trust. Then they try to trick you into sharing your login information or other personal deets online. Phishing is usually carried out over email. But it can also be done through phone calls (called "vishing" for voice phishing), text messaging (called "smishing" for SMS phishing), or via social media posts by sites that look suspiciously similar to ones you already use.[3]

Phishers usually target hundreds of people at once in the hope of catching one unsuspecting sucker who'll take the bait.

But what does phishing look like? Some attempts are obvious to spot—the emails, texts, or posts seem super general and often contain misspellings or weird sentence structures. Others are harder to identify, like when a scammer targets you directly and incorporates some of your personal information into the post. That's called spear-phishing. For example, let's say you get a Snapchat from your "Aunt Margie" who wants you to "wire $3,000 to yer Unkle Beevus in Gana rite away" and "text her yer bank akount number, wile yer at it." Sure, you do have an *Uncle Beavis* who happens to be in *Ghana* for business. But he has his own money. Clearly, he doesn't need money from his teenage relative. Plus, the *real* Aunt Margie can actually spell.

In order to avoid any form of phishing when you're using social media, follow these directions. Be careful about which posts you respond to. Read everything through the lens of a magnifying glass. Make sure you trust the source. Finally, before you click on an ad, respond to a Snapchat message, or enter your username and password into a site you find on social media, ask yourself some of the following questions:

- Does this post or site look professional and/or similar to other websites you know and trust? Is the company's real logo present? Is there a copyright signature at the bottom of the website's homepage? Do a fresh Google search of

When guarding against phishing and other scams, watch out for emails with lots of misspellings. It's a sure sign the sender's request isn't legit.

the site in question. Compare it to the link you clicked on in the post before taking any action or responding.

- What does the URL look like? Does it match the product's or company's name and information? Are there misspellings?
- Does the URL start with https:// with a tiny green padlock to the left of it? (That means the connection is secure.) If the https:// is missing or if the beginning of the link is red, avoid the page completely.
- Did you find the site in question by clicking on a link included in a post? If so, this isn't always safe. You can

check the destination of a link by hovering your mouse over it. If the URL does not match the link's anchor text or the post's stated destination, there is a good chance it could be bad news bears.

As always, it's best to be cautious. But if you *do* become a victim of phishing, don't freak out! You're not the first person to do so, and you won't be the last. Tell a parent, guardian, or teacher what happened right away. Then change the login password to your social media account immediately. If you're extra worried, you can also change your login on other social media accounts as well. Alert your friends, family, and the social media site's administrator. Phishers could be attacking other users, too.

Be Password Savvy

We've said it before and we'll say it again. Your social media profile is like your underwear drawer—some of the details in there are uber personal and should be kept private. One of the best ways to do so is to create extra strong passwords. They can be a four-digit number-only code or a much more complex letter-number-symbol combination. (Pro tip: your birthday, your home address, 1234, or "password" are all terrible ideas.) Here are a few tried-and-true tips on how to do so.

Use your thumbprint ID for sites that allow it. For sites that don't, longer passwords are better. The reason your noggin has trouble remembering them is the same reason they're hard for strangers to guess. Incorporate a mix of numbers, special characters (like % or *), and both lowercase and uppercase letters.

Try out different passwords for different social media sites. These logins should also be different from the password you use to access your email or your bank account. One idea is to think of a fun phrase only you will remember. Choose the first letter or first couple letters from each word in the phrase. Add some symbols or numbers and voila! Most important: mum's the word. Don't share your passwords with anyone—not even your crush or your BFF.

If you suspect your password or account has been hacked by "Aunt Margie," "Unkle Beevus," or some other nasty hacker with

Use lots of symbols in your passwords. They're harder to guess. Uppercase and lowercase letters are a smart choice, too.

Apps to Remember

Passwords are the bane of online existence. Remembering one password (let alone twenty!) can be annoyingly difficult. But the good news is there are loads of apps to help those of us nincompoops with foggy brains keep track. Some, like Dashlane and Keeper Password Manager & Digital Vault, cost money. But others, such as Last Pass, LogMeOnce, and 1Password are free and easy to use.[4] In addition to remembering your passwords, they can also help you choose smart ones, as well as sync your info between your phone, your tablet, and your other devices. Also, and we know this can sound crazy, but consider writing your passwords down on a piece of paper. Keep it hidden at home where only you can find it.

nothing else better to do, change your password immediately. Make sure you remember to list recovery information, like an alternate email or phone number, in case you forget your password or get locked out of your account in the future. Finally, use two-factor verification whenever possible. This usually involves one other factor on top of using your username and password or pin when logging in. For example, some banks require a username and password, plus an additional code that's texted to a phone, in order to access an account. Going through both steps may seem like one mongo headache. But it's an extra layer of security designed to make sure you're the only person who can access your account, even if someone knows your password.

Deactivate or Delete

For most teens (and many adults), social media is the place to be. It allows you to be creative and cool. You can communicate with your pals and connect with like-minded folks all over the world. But let's get straight for a second. Whether it's because your account has been hacked or you just need an extended minute without all that *noise*, sometimes a full-on social media detox is in order.

If this sounds at all familiar, join the club. In the last few years alone, tens of thousands of people young and old have taken a break from their social media accounts. Take these millennials, who expressed their thoughts on Mashable:

Twenty-two-year-old Austin took more than a month off from Twitter, Facebook, and Snapchat. "When I was thinking about New Year's resolutions, I decided I wanted to read more," he said. "I used to read a lot and when I thought about why I didn't anymore, I realized it was because I was killing time with social media instead of truly doing what I wanted to do." He claimed he might log back in again when he can "use social media more moderately."[1]

Twenty-five-year-old Amanda took more than three months off Facebook after her account was hacked. "I actually tried to find a way back on, but it was a really difficult process," she said. "Instead, I decided it was a good time to take a break, reported it to Facebook so they would shut down the account, and I've been without it ever since. I guess this was the push I needed to make a major change, even if it was a little dramatic."[2]

There are many reasons people take an extended or even a permanent break from social media. It's time-consuming. It's addictive. (Those JoJo Siwa or MattyBRaps videos? That's where it's at!) It can be tricky to compare your life to others', especially when you're not feeling on top of your game. In

Social media getting you down? Try taking a break from your feeds— or removing them from your devices altogether.

the worst scenario, maybe you're the target of a smutty smear campaign at school or your personal info has been stolen. Whatever your motivations are, definitive action needs to be taken.

According to tech experts, it's not possible to completely delete your online presence. But there is a sliding scale of ways to minimize your social media footprint. You know what they say: When it's time to cut the social media cord, *it's time to cut the cord*.

Go Incognito

Think of yourself as Susan Storm or the Invisible Man. Just because you're not physically *seen* on YouTube or Twitter, doesn't mean you're not actually there. Let's say you don't want to erase your social media presence altogether. After all, your situation isn't dire. And it's still fun to check in from time to time. Why not try cutting back on your usage just a smidge. Maybe drop the account you a) find the least enjoyable (after all, if you're not getting anything out of it, what's the point?) or b) think is the most addictive.

Another approach is to change your posting strategy. Rather than uploading videos and photos of yourself, or including personal or incriminating details in your posts, keep everything super general. Taking some sweet photos while on a family vacay in Alaska? Maybe leave the pics of you and your dorky brothers out of the slideshow you forward to your pals (and the world). Post scenery shots instead.

Lastly, just like it's important to straighten up your bedroom from time to time (You're welcome, Mom), it's also a good idea to clean house on social media. Purge any troublemakers from your Snapchat contact list. Defriend those bozos who refuse to stop vomiting their offensive political rants on your Facebook feed. Banish spam posters and suspicious-looking Instagram profiles alike. That means anyone who may not have your best interests in mind. Stores that send you annoying ads. Followers whose comments you don't agree with. With social media, the old adage holds true: better to be safe than sorry.

Deactivate and Delete

There are those rare times in life when a fun situation becomes decidedly *un-fun.* If someone has hacked your identity on

Cutting the Cord Feels Good!

When twenty-nine-year-old Gina Van Thomme deleted all of her social media accounts, at first she felt a vacuum where all the chatting, tweeting, following, and liking had been. But within just a few months, she noticed a huge difference in the way she felt. In short, her life basically did a 180. "For years, I used social media to try to find myself and, when I couldn't do that, to try to define myself," she said. "My decision to log off has improved so many things from my productivity to my relationships to my worldview."[3]

Offensive political posters, strangers with suspicious-looking profiles, and ad-heavy companies are all bad news. Unfollow! Unfriend! Trust us, it's liberating.

social media, maybe it's time to say adios for good. If so, it's probably smart to be decisive—and aggressive about wiping the slate clean. Here's a primer on what will happen if you kick some of your now-not-so-favorite social media accounts to the curb:

- Facebook: If you deactivate, you have the option of reactivating it later. If you go the "complete delete" route, your account will effectively be erased and all the posts and photos you uploaded will be gone after a few days. The company notes that friends can still see messages you might have sent them while your account was active.[4]
- Twitter: Once you deactivate your account, your name, username, and profile will permanently vanish. You can change your mind and reactivate it within thirty days.[5]

- Instagram: If you temporarily disable your account, your profile, photos, comments, and likes will be hidden until you reactivate it by logging back in. When you fully delete your account, your profile, photos, videos, comments, likes, and followers will be permanently removed. Deleted accounts cannot be reactivated. [6]

- Snapchat: Once you deactivate your account, your friends will not be able to contact or interact with you on Snapchat. After thirty days, your account will be permanently deleted. This means that your account, account settings, friends, Snaps, Chats, Story, device data, and location data in the company's main user database will be purged. The company notes that it does retain some data, even after your account is gone. This includes info about any purchases you may have made through the app.[7]

- YouTube: If you hide content from your YouTube channel, your channel name, videos, likes, subscriptions, and subscribers will be made private. All your comments and replies will be permanently deleted. Your account data on other Google properties will not be removed. If you choose to permanently delete your channel, its videos, comments, messages, playlists, and history will all vanish. The company notes that brand accounts can hide their content, but they can't hide or delete their channels. Channels can't be deleted using a mobile device. [8]

Staying empowered on social media means being mindful of what you post—and how you react to what others post. Post with intention. Repost with caution. Stay safe and have fun!

One Final Reminder...

Your time on social media should be the bees' knees. Ideally, it should never make you feel self-conscious or, worse, self-destructive. But like most tools on your beauty counter, the platforms function best when they're used properly.

Do onto others as you would have them do onto you. Be smart. Remain safe. And remember that underwear drawer: Keep your personal 411 protected.

Chapter Notes

Introduction

1. Monica Anderson and Jingjing Jiang, "Teens, Social Media & Technology 2018," Pewinternet.org, May 31, 2018, http://www.pewinternet.org/2018/05/31/teens-social-media-technology-2018/.

Chapter 1: The Private vs. Public You

1. Ana Homayoun, "The Secret Social Media Lives of Teenagers," *New York Times*, June 7, 2017, https://www.nytimes.com/2017/06/07/well/family/the-secret-social-media-lives-of-teenagers.html.
2. Ibid.
3. Ibid.
4. Ibid.

Chapter 2: Marketing and Data Mining

1. Monica Anderson and Jingjing Jiang, "Teens, Social Media & Technology 2018," Pewinternet.org, May 31, 2018, http://www.pewinternet.org/2018/05/31/teens-social-media-technology-2018/.
2. "Data Policy," Instagram.com, retrieved October 12, 2018, https://help.instagram.com/155833707900388.
3. Neil J. Rubenking, "Viruses, Spyware, and Malware: What's the Difference?" PCmag.com, August 21, 2018, https://www.pcmag.com/article2/0,2817,2379663,00.asp.
4. Sheera Frenkel and Katie Benner, "To Stir Discord in 2016, Russians Turned Most Often to Facebook," *New York Times*, February 17, 2018, https://www.nytimes.

com/2018/02/17/technology/indictment-russian-tech-facebook.
html?module=inline.

Chapter 3: Hacking, Phishing, and Identity Theft

1. Mike Isaac and Sheera Frenkel, "Facebook Security Breach Exposes Accounts of 50 Million Users," *New York Times*, September 28, 2018, https://www.nytimes.com/2018/09/28/ technology/facebook-hack-data-breach.html?emc=edit_ na_20180928&nl=breaking-news&nlid=16028460ing-news&ref=headline.

2. "Facts + Statistics: Identity Theft and Cybercrime," Insurance Information Institute, retrieved September 24, 2018, https:// www.iii.org/fact-statistic/facts-statistics-identity-theft-and-cybercrime.

3. Nena Giandomenico, "What Is Spear-phishing? Defining and Differentiating Spear-phishing from Phishing," DataInsider, September 19, 2018, https://digitalguardian.com/blog/what-is-spear-phishing-defining-and-differentiating-spear-phishing-and-phishing.

4. Neil J. Rubenking, "The Best Free Password Managers of 2018," PCMag.com, October 5, 2018, https://www.pcmag.com/ article2/0,2817,2475964,00.asp.

Chapter 4: Deactivate or Delete

1. Chloe Bryan, "8 People Confess Why They Finally Deleted Social Media," Mashable, February 11, 2018, https:// mashable.com/2018/02/11/reasons-to-delete-social-media/#_ I5qMQhawmq6.

2. Ibid.

3. Gina Van Thomme, "I Deleted All My Social Media Accounts Last Year. Here's How My Life Has Changed," *HuffPost,* July 17, 2018, https://www.huffingtonpost.com/entry/deleting-social-media_us_5b4cd4d9e4b0e7c958fe2233.

4. "Deactivating or Deleting Your Account," Facebook.com, retrieved September 24, 2018, https://www.facebook.com/help/250563911970368?helpref=hc_global_nav.

5. "How to Deactivate Your Account," Twitter.com, retrieved September 24, 2018, https://help.twitter.com/en/managing-your-account/how-to-deactivate-twitter-account.

6. "Delete Your Account," Instagram.com, retrieved September 24, 2018, https://help.instagram.com/370452623149242.

7. "Delete My Account," Snapchat.com, retrieved September 24, 2018, https://support.snapchat.com/en-US/a/delete-my-account1.

8. "Delete or Hide Your YouTube Channel," YouTube.com, retrieved September 24, 2018, https://support.google.com/youtube/answer/55759?hl=en.

Glossary

anchor text The text that appears highlighted in a link and can be clicked to open a web page.

app A software program that is usually used on a smartphone or a tablet computer. ("App" is short for application.)

cookies A type of tracking software that stores screen names, preference settings, and other information on a computer.

digital footprint The evidence of a person's online activity.

geotagging Adding a sender's or poster's geographical information to various media, such as photos, texts, or videos.

hacking Breaking into a software system or social media account.

identity theft Stealing and using a person's private identifying information, usually for financial gain.

malware Software that is intended to damage or disable computers and computer systems.

phishing The illegal practice of posing as a reputable company or individual and sending fake emails, messages, or posts in order to get the recipient to reveal personal information, such as passwords and credit card numbers.

scareware Bad computer programs designed to trick a user into downloading unnecessary and potentially dangerous software, such as fake antivirus protection.

spyware Software that allows users to obtain information about another person's computer habits by secretly accessing data on their hard drive.

thumbprint ID When you log in to a website or social media account using your thumbprint.

troll A person who posts offensive or provocative content online, or someone who harasses someone else for offensive reasons.

two-factor verification The practice of using two separate methods to log in to an online account, usually using a password and one other method.

Further Reading

Books

Fromm, Megan. *Media Literacy: Privacy and Digital Security.* New York, NY: Rosen Publishing, 2015.

January, Brendan. *Information Insecurity: Privacy under Siege.* Minneapolis, MN: Twenty-First Century Books, 2016.

McKee, Jonathan. *The Teen's Guide to Social Media...and Mobile Devices: 21 Tips to Wise Posting in an Insecure World.* Uhrichsville, OH: Shiloh Run Press, 2017.

Websites

Google: Interland
beinternetawesome.withgoogle.com/en/interland
A super fun site that teaches kids and teens about digital literacy and internet safety through four games.

National Cyber Security Alliance
staysafeonline.org
Provides resources and tips for kids, teens, and adults on how to stay safe online.

Safekids: Kids' Rules for Online Safety
https://www.safekids.com/kids-rules-for-online-safety
Find helpful rules for safe internet use.

Index